A Magician Among the Spirits

Poems by
Charles Rammelkamp

BLUE LIGHT PRESS ◆ 1ST WORLD PUBLISHING

1st WORLD
PUBLISHING

SAN FRANCISCO ◆ FAIRFIELD ◆ DELHI

Winner, 2022 Blue Light Poetry Prize
A Magician Among the Spirits

BLUE LIGHT PRESS
www.bluelightpress.com
bluelightpress@aol.com

1ST WORLD PUBLISHING
PO Box 2211
Fairfield, IA 52556
www.1stworldpublishing.com

BOOK & COVER DESIGN
Melanie Gendron
melaniegendron999@gmail.com

COVER PHOTO
Houdini, "American photographer," circa 1899, Library of Congress

AUTHOR PHOTO
Abby Rammelkamp

FIRST EDITION

Library of Congress Cataloging-in-Publication Data

ISBN: 978-1-4218-3531-0

This book is for Abby

"You don't take nothin' with you but your soul."
"The Ballad of John and Yoko"

"The world is full of magic things,
patiently waiting for our senses to grow sharper."
– W.B. Yeats

Table of Contents

PART ONE: Inventing an Identity

Alternative Facts 1
My Father Flees 2
Inspiration 4
Running Away to Join the Circus 5
Dash 7
Mama 8
A Star Is Born 9
Projea 10
Publicity 11
Escape 13
The Hungry Years 14
Buster 16
Jailbreak! 17
Houdini Amazes Detectives 18
Scotland Yard 19
The Queen 20
Landsman 22
The Siberian Transport Cell 24
Homage 26
Advertising 28
Home 29
Books 30
Underwater Escape 31
Suspense 32
The Milk Can Escape 33
The Chinese Water Torture Cell 34
Escaping from the Assassin's Cell 35
First 36

PART TWO: And Then Everything Changed

My Mama 41
Burying Mama 43
Soliloquy 44
Aftermath 45
Spirits 46
Death Wish 47
Houdinizing 48
Special Powers 49
The Rabbis' Sons' Benevolent Association 51
The Silver Screen 52
The Master of Mystery 53
The Movies 54
My Wild Oat 55
Elementary 57
Spiritualism 58
Meeting the Doyles 60
Mediums 61
Ectoplasm 62
The American Mission 63
The Séance 65
The Rift 67
A Psychic Diogenes 68
The *Scientific American* 70
The Blonde Witch of Lime Street 73
Margery at the Charlesgate 74

CODA: Escape

Alternative Facts II 79
The Great Escape 81

Acknowledgements 83
About the Author 85

PART ONE:

Inventing an Identity

Alternative Facts

In London, at the U.S. embassy,
I surrendered my old passport,
the one I'd acquired in New York
before we crossed the Atlantic
on the S.S. *Kensington,* May, 1900.

The document identified me
as a naturalized citizen,
born in Budapest, Hungary, in 1874.
The new passport, issued in London,
declared me a native American,
born in Appleton, Wisconsin.

I also changed my occupation
from "actor" to "artiste,"
my eyes from brown to blue,
and – why not? – added a few inches
to my height, now listed as 5'6".

I am an American!
As Walt Whitman once asked,
Do I contradict myself?
Very well then, I contradict myself.
I contain multitudes!

My Father Flees

They Americanized our name
when Papa came to America,
from "Weisz" to "Weiss" –
already the facts elude
the straitjacket of "reality" –
a rabbi, ordained at only twenty-two in 1851.
Studied law at the University of Pest,
his occupation listed as "legal counselor"
on my Hungarian birth certificate.

I was just two years old
when he left us behind in Hungary.
The story I learned:
he'd fought a duel
over an anti-Semitic slur,
killing a prince, fleeing to London
before coming to America.

Rabbi in Appleton, Wisconsin,
when he sent for us two years later,
he led services in a building on College Avenue
(Lawrence University, second co-ed college
in America, Appleton's pride)
while the congregation raised money
for a new shul.

But he fell out of favor with the *machers* –
too old-fashioned, didn't speak English,
resisted assimilation, too attached
to his Old World ways.

So Rabbi Mayer Samuel Weiss,
now with seven kids to care for,
out of a job, moved us to Milwaukee,
where he offered his services
as a *mohel* and a *shochet* –
various cuts of meat
that never added up to rent.

When we moved to New York,
Papa's luck didn't change –
a scholar, not an escape artist.
He wound up cutting linings
for a necktie manufacturer,
forced to sell his precious books,
including the *Code of Maimonides*,
dying after an operation
for cancer of the tongue.

Inspiration

A failure? No, he was an inspiration.
He learned in America
you have the freedom to fail,
escape is always an option,
but he never gave up.

One of the first rabbis
in the American Midwest,
noted Talmudic scholar,
a writer of speculative disquisitions,
Papa never accepted defeat.

Father of seven, he *was* an inspiration,
not that Bess and I ever had children,
and my sainted Mama Cecilia did all the child-rearing:
still, he taught me to value education and hard work.
I was a newsboy in Milwaukee at age eight,
flogging the *Milwaukee Journal*,
a shoeshine boy, too,
performed at nine for the first time,
a trapeze artist in a kids' circus,
Ehrich, the Prince of Air.

How it crushed me to see his sorrow
when he had to sell his volumes
of rabbinical literature to support our family,
and years later, I got the *Code of Maimonides* back
from Bernard Drachman, the rabbi
who'd officiated at my bar mitzvah,
making a $500 donation to his synagogue,
securing my memorial to my father.

Running Away to Join the Circus

Papa lost his job
at Zion Reform Jewish Congregation
three months before we all became American citizens,
but it was three years later, in Milwaukee,
when I was thirteen,
my older brother Hermie died, tuberculosis,
and I just couldn't take all the tragedy any more –
the mourning, the poverty, the hunger, the failure:
I needed to escape.

Papa's son by his first marriage,
Hermie's mother'd died in childbirth,
Papa re-marrying later that year,
Cecilia Steiner, my mother,
thirteen years younger than he.

Hermie'd cared for us all on the SS *Frisia*,
when we made the trip to America,
just fourteen then, but four-year-old me
looked up to him as a kind of god.

So I just had to escape; story of my life.
My destination? Galveston, Texas,
but I only made it as far as Kansas City,
and soon enough I was back in Wisconsin,
in Delavan, fifty miles south of Milwaukee,
where any number of circuses wintered
before going back out on tour come spring.

When Papa sought his failure in New York,
I was the first to join him,
a roominghouse on the Upper East Side,

all of us moving to a cold-water flat
on East 75th Street,
when Mama and the others joined us,
he and I working side by side
in the necktie sweatshop.

Dash

Closest of my siblings?
That would have to be Dash,
my younger brother Theodore,
born Ferenc Dezső Weisz –
how malleable identity is!
How we escape to who we really are!

When my first magic partner, Jacob Hyman,
moved on, a guy I knew from the cutting bench –
we'd first performed at the Pastime Athletic Club
on East 69th – I recruited my younger brother.

Together, as the Brothers Houdini,
we toured the Northeast and Midwest,
performing in dime museums, beer halls,
medicine shows, cheap variety theaters,
working alongside snake charmers, strongmen,
belly dancers, blackface minstrels, sideshow freaks.

We even performed on the midway
at the 1893 World's Fair in Chicago,
calling ourselves the Modern Monarchs of Mystery –
sleight of hand, card tricks, mind-reading,
and my very first escape trick, the Metamorphosis,
breaking out of a locked box, hands tied behind me.

We broke up a year later
after I met Bess on Coney Island,
she in the Floral Sisters, a song-and-dance act.
Bess and I married three weeks later,
began performing as the Great Houdinis.

But I encouraged Dash to take up escapology,
even gave him his new stage name: Hardeen.

Mama

It was my sainted mother
to whom I was most devoted,
all my life, even married to Bess.

How my heart broke when Papa died,
and I heard her anguished wail, "Weiss! Weiss!
You've left me with your children!
What have you done?"

I was eighteen then. I'd vowed
to Papa on his death bed
Mama would never want for anything,
a promise he'd demanded
during our deepest Milwaukee misery.

After I became famous, wealthy as Rockefeller,
I bought a Harlem brownstone –
278 West 113th Street, always known as "278" –
where I installed Mother,
sending her to the Catskills every summer
to escape the sultry city summer,
breathe in the salubrious mountain air.

A Star Is Born

I started my career as Eric the Great;
it's what I called myself
when Jacob Hyman and I first performed.
We'd practiced together after work,
on sweatshop breaks, daring each other
to perform in public, before an audience.

We both admired Jean-Eugene Robert Houdin,
the Frenchman known as the first modern magician,
who'd died a few years before I was born.
I'd come across a second-hand copy of his memoirs.
A Conjuror's Confessions became my bible,
textbook, manual, gospel.

Jacob suggested the stage name:
adding the "i" at the end added mystery,
so it felt like counterfeit.
Thus we became the Houdini Brothers,
a name I'd keep when my real brother Dash
took Jacob's place after he'd moved on.

We earned just enough performing
that I realized I could escape the sweatshop,
that tedious job cutting fabric,
devote myself full-time to performing magic.

Harry? A short step from the name
I was already known by,
"Ehrie" a diminutive of Eric.
Harry Houdini was born.

Projea

The early days were rough,
but we loved it.
In the summer of 1895,
Bess and I joined
the Welsh Brothers Circus Troupe,
mainly playing venues in Pennsylvania.
They paid us $25 a week to perform
every big-top entertainment you could think of –
hypnotism, clowning, song-and-dance, acrobatics.

I even appeared as a sideshow freak,
Projea, the Wild Man of Mexico.
With gusto I shook the bars of my cage,
hurling myself against them time and again,
snarling and bellowing at the crowd,
reveling in the big round eyes of kids
cowering into their parents' embrace.
I even gnawed at chunks of raw meat,
blood and juices dripping down my jaws.

I learned so much from the sideshow acts,
the fat lady, the one-armed violinist,
the man who walked over hot coals.
As Robert-Houdin wrote,
"A conjurer is an *actor*
playing the role of a magician."

Publicity

After the Welsh Brothers flopped
like a fish on a dry dock,
one of my cousins on Mama's side
convinced me to buy a share
in a traveling burlesque show.
Why not? I was only twenty-one,
open for adventure,
an escape into another kind of life.

So that's how Bess and I got involved
with American Gaiety Girls, owners
of an itinerant titty show,
going around New England
with strip-teasers belting out
bawdy songs, dirty jokes delivered
with a wink and a leer,
peddling erotic fantasies like lottery tickets.

My magic act got lost in all that flesh,
but one night in Manchester, New Hampshire,
just as I was preparing for the Metamorphosis trick,
I got the idea to use handcuffs,
instead of ropes, to bind my hands.

In Gloucester, Mass., our next stop,
I went to the police station
to show off my new skill to the cops.
The *Gloucester Daily News* covered the caper
in the news section, mentioning
we'd be performing that evening.

We did the same thing in Woonsocket,
and a few days later in Holyoke.

The *Daily Democrat* there reported
I shed handcuffs as if they were merely strings
wound around my wrists.

Despite the free publicity,
American Gaiety Girls couldn't escape
from inevitable failure, but at least
we learned a valuable lesson in marketing.

Escape

Marco the Monarch of Mystery,
aka, Edward Dooley, owner of the Marco Company,
took me and Bess on
for a tour of the Maritime Provinces
in the spring of 1896,
but the company went bust after only a month,
playing to empty houses in Nova Scotia and New Brunswick.
In Halifax, a sheriff broke up our last performance
to take possession of Marco's equipment
on the creditors' behalf.

Only a week before I'd performed my first jailbreak,
stripped down to my bathing suit,
handcuffed, locked away in a Halifax prison cell
with heavy iron doors, brick walls a foot thick.
The police only found out I'd escaped
when the Queen Hotel concierge called,
asking for the safe return my clothes.

In Saint John, on the coast,
the police chief asked me to test
a new device his brother-in-law, the superintendent
of New Brunswick Provincial Lunatic Asylum,
used to restrain his inmates:
my introduction to the straitjacket!
I watched a poor devil in a padded cell
wriggling like a snake on the floor,
attempting to shed his restraining skin.
The self-crowned Handcuff King,
I had to test it for myself,
spent a week with one, on loan,
incorporating it into my act.

For a failure, that Canadian tour
was a mighty success!

The Hungry Years

Bess and I appeared as a comedy duo for a while,
calling ourselves the Rahners, her maiden name;
I did card tricks as a character called Cardo.
As Professor Marat, I hypnotized her onstage
as part of Doctor Hill's medicine show,
a slick operator who sold a patent elixir
he claimed could cure
headache, constipation, impotence and more.

We also did a mind-reading act,
Bess billed as Mademoiselle Houdini,
blindfolded onstage but
"reading the minds" of audience members
to accurately recite the dates on coins,
which of course I spilled to her in code.

With the California Concert Company,
we also conducted "spiritualistic séances,"
me Professor Harry Houdini, the Great Mystifier,
Bess Mlle. Beatrice Houdini,
the Celebrated Psycrometic Clairvoyant,
hinting at scandals, extramarital affairs,
unsolved murders. ("The killer is among us.")

Through it all, I always sent Mama
a portion of our weekly earnings,
honoring the promise I'd made to my father.
We always stayed at her apartment on East 69th
when we came back home from touring.

At the end of 1898, we almost threw in the towel.
We sent flyers to theater managers but got no offers.

I advertised Professor Harry Houdini's School of Magic
in the backs of catalogues, but nobody enrolled.
We had no choice but to go back out on the road.

Buster

I liked to tell the story
I gave little Joe Keaton his nickname,
Buster. He was just a tyke
when Bess and I toured the Midwest
with Doctor Thomas' medicine show,
the California Concert Company, as it was called.

We became friends with Joe and Myra,
who had a vaudeville act called The Two Keatons,
slapstick comedy, later called The Three Keatons,
 when Buster became part of the act at the age of three.

They'd met as performers in Myra's dad's medicine show,
traveling around the Oklahoma Territory,
before going out on their own.
Little Buster'd been birthed in Piqua, Kansas,
where their show was when Myra went into labor.

The story we told –
Buster, too, though he wasn't yet two when it happened –
was how the little guy took a tumble
down a flight of stairs but shrugged it off, unscathed.
"That was a real buster!" I exclaimed
to the shaken parents, relieved
their son hadn't been seriously injured.
The name stuck. But the story shifted:
some people said George Pardey really gave him the name,
but Buster stuck to our story once I became famous.
Does it really matter?

I always loved Buster in *The General*.
That deadpan expression always cracked me up,
the emotions he concealed,
the circumstances escaped.

Jailbreak!

It felt like busting out of a cell,
our big beer hall break in St. Paul,
early spring in Minnesota still winter-cold.
We were performing in the Palm Garden Beer Hall
when in walked Martin Beck
with a party of theater managers.
Beck oversaw the western Orpheum vaudeville circuit,
in cahoots with Keith and Albee,
who monopolized vaudeville
back east and soon enough nationwide.

Beck sent several pairs of handcuffs backstage.
I escaped without breaking a sweat.
A few weeks later, he sent me a telegram.
"You can open Omaha March twenty-sixth,
sixty dollars. Will make a proposition
for all next season."

No more dime museums or beer halls
for Bess and me!
We'd made the big time!
An escape into success!

Houdini Amazes Detectives

Beck recognized escape amazed the audience,
not the conjuring or the card tricks,
but breaking free from restraints,
eluding disaster, a step ahead of catastrophe,
so often a matter of life and death.

My police station stunt, the press coverage,
cops in awe, scratching their heads –
you can't buy that kind of advertising,
you can't make it up.
San Francisco, Chicago, Boston,
at jailhouses all over the country,
surrounded by uniforms, stripped naked,
poked, prodded, probed with fingers and instruments,
then handcuffed, shackled, bound,
festooned with chains like a Christmas tree,
locked up in a cell, keyholes sealed,
I always found my way out,
and the newspaper headlines spelled it all out.

After a year I was making $400 a week,
more than half Papa's annual salary at the Appleton shul.
I'd escaped the shackles of poverty.

MANACLES DO NOT HOLD HIM!
The Kansas City Times shouted in black and white.

Scotland Yard

At the turn of the century, in May,
Bess and I boarded the SS *Kensington*,
bound for Southampton.
We'd taken lodgings in Bloomsbury,
a couple of blocks from the British Museum,
only to discover the agent who'd promised
advanced bookings was a liar.

Meetings with theatrical agents a bust,
we finally met the manager
of the Alhambra Theatre in Leicester Square,
Slater, who sneered at handcuff escapes,
until I won him over when Scotland Yard
shackled me like Samson to a pillar
with a pair of regulation British cuffs,
and I removed them faster
than you could say fish and chips.

The newspapers ate it up,
marveling at the way I shed every restraint –
cuffs, leg irons, chains, containers –
scattering them all across the stage floor,
unlocked, useless.

My two-week run extended through August,
I always received thunderous curtain calls,
thousands in the audience roaring their approval.
Soon I was hauling in $1000 a week!

The Queen

"*Tateleh*," Mama called me – a Yiddish endearment,
"Little Papa."
The textbook Freudians wrote
I had an Oedipal Complex, citing
her custom of holding me to her breast,
even as an adult, the sound of her heartbeat
soothing as milk suckled from a nipple.
Why sully our devotion to one another?

I was rich now, wanted to spoil her,
her sixtieth birthday coming in June.
Back for an engagement at the Alhambra,
I noticed a gown designed for Queen Victoria
in the window of a London shop.
She'd only recently died.

I bought the dress for fifty pounds –
on the shopkeeper's condition
it never be worn in Great Britain.
When I walked out of that shop with the dress,
I would not have changed places
with any crowned head in Europe.

Mama came to Hamburg in June,
where I was performing at the Hansa Theater,
then we took a train to Budapest,
the city we'd left over two decades earlier,
the celebration planned for the Grand Hotel Royal.

How my heart warmed to see
various friends and relatives kneel,
pay homage to my mother,
enthroned in a carved and gilded chair,
wearing the dress I had bought her!

Back in the United States, Mama received
regular cables from the monarchs of Europe,
kings and queens sending their greetings.
Of course, I was the one who sent them,
a bit of my Houdini magic,
but I really believe she thought them real.

Landsman

I have never been ashamed
to acknowledge that I was a Jew,
and I never will be.
True, after my bar mitzvah,
I rarely set foot in a synagogue again,
but I always recited Kaddish
on the anniversary of my father's death,
no matter where I might be.

All across Europe, I heard the Jew Haters,
what awful things they said,
not realizing I was Jewish myself.

Or did they?
In Germany, performing to a packed house
at the Central Theater in Dresden,
I was ordered to appear at police headquarters
in Berlin, the Polizeipräsidium Alexanderplatz,
Germany's Scotland Yard,
where I was stripped to my underwear,
my arms pinned behind me with an array
of handcuffs, thumbscrews and finger locks,
my mouth taped shut, secured by leg irons.

Six minutes later I emerged
from under the sheet they tossed over me,
dumping the load of iron on the table.

But this was just the beginning.
In Cologne I was accused of fraud.
I sued for slander but was forced
to reveal my technique

in order to save my honor.
But at least I won the case.

Russia was even worse.
I performed in Kishinev and saw
firsthand traces of the bloody pogroms,
scores dead, hundreds wounded.
Bess, of course, was Roman Catholic,
and we traveled around Russia
"as a Christian couple."

The Siberian Transport Cell

I'd opened at the Yar, the popular Moscow dinner theater
frequented by high society aristocrats,
where Rasputin would later get drunk,
cause a scandal grabbing the gypsy dancers,
boasting about his relations with Alexandra,
but I wanted the publicity of a prison break,
and what better venue than Butyrskaya prison,
the Moscow landmark built
during the reign of Catherine the Great?

But the Police Chief, a man named Lebedev,
suggested the Siberian Transport Cell instead,
the "safe on wheels" they used to transport
political prisoners to Siberia,
a four-week journey in an unheated box.
I agreed, but only if he'd sign an affidavit
if I successfully escaped. Good press!

I was stripped naked, searched head to toe,
led across the freezing prison courtyard,
manacled in heavy irons, locked inside
the transport cell – after it had been searched.
If I failed to escape, they told me,
I'd have to stay in the cell until we reached Sackolin,
where the only key was kept that unlocked the cell.

Within an hour I was out, walked into Lebedev's office,
drenched in sweat but free.
Only, Lebedev didn't provide the affidavit,
so no newspaper ran the story.

Still, word got around; it always does.

My tour was extended. I even performed
at Palace Kleinmichel for Grand Duke Sergei Alexandrovich,
who'd later be killed when a revolutionary
threw a bomb into his carriage.
(He'd overseen Moscow's expulsion of the Jews.)

I never went back to Russia.
The whole country felt like some sort of mild prison,
getting out alive itself an escape.

Homage

I'd always admired my predecessors in magic
as well as some contemporaries, made a point
of having photographs taken with them,
Howard Thurston, Harry Kellar,
Cardini, Chung Link Soo and others.

In France, I wrote Robert-Hardin's widowed daughter-in-law
to seek permission to pay her a visit,
lay a wreath on the grave,
but she refused.

I went anyway,
a four-hour train trip from Paris
to the town of Blois, in the Loire Valley,
his birthplace and the site of his grave,
January 28, 1902.

The following year I sought Wiljalba Frikell,
one of Robert-Houdin's contemporaries, 87,
living in seclusion near Dresden.
He refused an interview.
I showed up anyway, unannounced.
A servant turned me away at the door.

But I persisted, pleading my case,
and when I was in Russia,
he sent me a note requesting a brand of Russian tea.
I sent it to him and got the invitation.

That October, I had a month-long engagement
at the Central Theater in Dresden.
I went to Frikell's house on the appointed day.

A woman greeted me at the door.
"You are being waited for," she said and led
us to a room where the old man lay dead,
dressed in a suit, his memorabilia around him.
He'd died from a heart attack just two hours earlier.

At the funeral, I placed a wreath on his grave.

Advertising

A fellow magician, T. Nelson Downs –
also known as the "King of Koins" –
once called me "the P.T. Barnum of today."
Fair enough. But if I didn't promote myself,
who would? Sure, the impresarios had an interest,
but for them I was just one act among many.

For my premiere at the Paris Olympia,
I hired seven bald men to sit in a row at a café,
one letter of my name painted on each pate.
They bowed reverentially to passers-by,
removed their hats in sequence, spelling H-O-U-D-I-N-I.

I still got my free publicity –
shedding the cuffs, breaking out of jails,
the press covering every stunt –
but I also turned to print.
America's Sensational Perplexer, the title
of my twelve-page pamphlet proclaiming
my jaw-dropping accomplishments,
sold or distributed for free by the tens of thousands,
making me the best advertised man that ever
crossed the vaudeville stage in all of Europe.
And it did the trick! Sold tickets, boosted attendance,
not to mention made me richer!

Besides, I knew I was the greatest.

Home

I made my name in Europe,
fame and fortune my reward.
I especially liked London,
but America was my home.

I left England in early summer, 1904,
for a three-month vacation,
buying a Humber motorcar,
shipping it across the Atlantic.

But when we got back to New York,
I thought it was time to settle down.
That's when I bought the Harlem brownstone,
also a 68-acre farm near Stamford, Connecticut.

I also bought a family burial plot
in a Jewish cemetery in Queens,
where I had the remains of Papa, Mama's mother,
and my half-brother Herman transferred.

Home is a final resting place, isn't it?
I'd spend more time in Europe
over the next ten years, until war broke out,
but now I had roots, even while I remained restless.

We'd all call the brownstone "278,"
more than a dozen rooms on four floors,
my mother, mother-in-law, various siblings
living there. Leo even had his doctor's office.

True, I'd only be there off and on
over the following decades, but
I had the finest private house any magician
ever had the great fortune to possess.

Books

I never got the formal academic training
my father did – religion, the law –
but he did instill in me a love
of books and learning –
People of the Book –
as well as his fear of failure,
the impulse to escape.

During that first European tour,
I began poking around old bookshops,
collecting odd volumes, the history of magic,
the careers of the early magicians,
almost anything involving the theater.

As time went on, I'd have the finest,
most complete collection of magic.
If all the libraries in the world
put all their magical literature under one roof,
they would still never match mine!

Underwater Escape

"A Shackle-Breaking Match under Water,"
the *New York Times* headline screamed,
my publicity stunt portrayed as a "challenge"
between me and Jacques Boudini, my "rival."
"The victor was to get $500," the story concluded.

September 20, 1905 – my first underwater escape,
ferried out to the middle of the Atlantic Basin,
Brooklyn piers and shipbuilding yards all around us,
Boudini and I shackled with cuffs on ankles and hands,
ropes girdling our waists, lowered into the briny water.

Of course, I freed myself in a couple of minutes,
though to the witnesses on the boat,
each second under the waves was an eternity.
Boudini? Not so lucky – not as skilled.
He had to be hauled out, still in cuffs.

I'd had an extra-large tub installed at 278,
to perfect this new death-defying twist to my act,
underwater escapes, which I'd enhance
with the passing years – the 1906 20-foot plunge
from the Belle Isle Bridge into the Detroit River,
the 1907 Weighlock Bridge dive into the Erie Canal.

I never did get that $500 prize, but what I did get –
so much more valuable,
to judge from the size of the audiences
that flocked to my performances.

Suspense

The easiest way to attract a crowd
is to let it be known
that at a given time and place
someone is going to attempt something
that in the event of failure
will mean certain death.

The newspapers were full of those stories.
The *London Daily Mail* ran a piece
about a "so-called Handcuff King"
who jumped manacled from a bridge in 1909.
"He failed in the attempt and was drowned."

Always my crowds were huge and enthusiastic.
They all wanted to see me succeed.
Unless I failed.
They thronged to see me in Pittsburgh,
leaping into the Allegheny from the Seventh Street Bridge;
in Los Angeles into the lake at MacArthur Park;
from the Harvard Bridge into the Charles, in Boston;
into the Schuylkill River (the "Sure-kill")
from the Market Street Bridge in Philly.

April in Paris, 1909,
I jumped into the Seine from the roof
of the morgue on the Ile de la Cité.

Locked up and loaded down when I submerged,
I never failed to emerge from the water free.

The Milk Can Escape

I needed a way to replicate onstage
the death-defying thrill of my bridge jumps.
I'd be strapped in a straitjacket
in plain sight of the audience,
straining in their seats, craning their necks,
while I writhed and thrashed before them,
wriggling like some monstrous serpent,
finally freeing myself, sweaty and exhausted.

I embellished my packing crate escape –
the "nailed up in a box gag," as I called it in private –
which I'd introduced in Essen, Germany, in 1902.
Now I was jammed, manacled, into airtight containers
filled with water, so the clock became a factor,
racing against time or else risk drowning.

On the vaudeville circuit,
they started calling my act the "Death and Resurrection Show."
I called my latest trick the "Milk Can Escape."
Lowered into a galvanized iron can onstage,
nothing on but my bathing suit,
hands fastened by cuffs, the tank filled with water,
assistants secured the top with six padlocks.
One of my assistants, faithful Franz Kukol
(he and his wife even named one of their kids Harry Houdini),
brandished an ax in case I didn't make it out,
while the orchestra played "Asleep in the Deep."

Imagine the audience holding their own breath
while the seconds ticked by,
two minutes, three – an eternity.
Then *bang!* I emerged, dripping,
heaving deep ragged breaths,
the can still padlocked.
The crowd went nuts.

The Chinese Water Torture Cell

I kept making improvements to the Milk Can trick.
I designed the world's largest stopwatch,
so the audience could endure the agony tick by tick;
I substituted cow's milk and beer for the water;
I had the can placed in a gigantic wooden chest,
circled with steel bands and padlocked.

But my greatest trick? The one I had copyrighted,
so no other magician could perform it?
Sheer genius: I staged just one performance
of my drama, *Challenged; or Houdini Upside Down*
in 1911 at the Hippodrome in Southampton,
to an audience of one,
so I could legally prevent imitators from stealing it.

But I didn't debut the Water Torture Cell
until 1912, in Berlin, at Circus Busch.
My assistants, wearing brocaded uniforms,
winched me up, bound, feet shackled,
then lowered me headfirst into a water-filled tank,
as if into a glass coffin.
Audiences roared their relieved approval
when I at last emerged, drenched, eyes bloodshot, gasping.

I'd perform this trick for the rest of my life,
at the Cardiff Empire in London,
at Hammerstein's Roof Garden in Times Square,
everywhere we went around the world.
It really was like a resurrection!

The ultimate escape!

Escaping from the Assassin's Cell

About the time I introduced the Chinese Water Torture Cell,
I gave up on the jailbreaks.
I'd been doing them for almost two decades;
they were getting to be tedious.

They'd become more elaborate over time,
police forces all over challenging me,
determined to be the ones
to thwart the great Houdini once and for all.
The Somerset Street prison in Boston –
aka, the Tombs – boasted the cells were "escape proof,"
but in sixteen minutes I was out of there,
calling the police superintendent
from my dressing room at Keith's Theater on Tremont Street.

But my favorite jail escape
happened in Washington, D.C.,
when I broke out of the same cell
Charles Guiteau was locked up in a quarter century before,
the man who assassinated President Garfield in 1882,
a brick cell with iron bars on "murderers row,"
in the federal prison on the Potomac.
Not only did I escape almost immediately,
but I switched each of the other nine prisoners
into different cells!

Oh yes: I was still naked at the time.

First

I was always a daredevil –
handcuffs, jailbreaks, straitjackets, bridge jumps –
but above all I wanted to be *first* –
first in my profession, first among magicians.

So when Louis Blériot piloted an airplane
across the English Channel, July, 1909,
I was determined to fly! How could I be left behind?
When I saw a German aviator circling Hamburg
in a Voisin biplane, I decided to buy one.

My first flight, though, in France, in November,
not quite the triumph I'd envisioned:
brief, bumpy, the landing a bit abrupt –
smashed the propeller all to hell.
I took out a $25,000 life insurance policy!

I'd just been offered $1,000 per week
to perform in Melbourne and Sydney,
so in January I had my Voisin disassembled, loaded with us
on the RMS *Malwa* in Marseilles, bound for Adelaide.

It was summer down under and hot as blazes.
I did a bridge jump into the Yarra River, from Queens Bridge,
while my mechanic, Brassac, reassembled the Voisin.
But the engine wasn't ready for nearly a month!
I almost went mad!

Finally, on March 18, I made three flights,
the final one lasting three and a half minutes,
two miles, a hundred feet above ground!
The Aerial League of Australia officially credited me
 with making the first airplane flight in Australia!

First! I was the *first*. And it was sweet.
As I exulted to the reporter from the *Argus* newspaper,
"Freedom and exhilaration, that's what it is!"
Synonyms for "escape."

PART TWO:

And Then Everything Changed

My Mama

Leaving Mama at home when we went on tour
became such an agony, she so frail.
She'd started telling me, when we parted at the pier,
she was afraid it was the last time we'd see each other.
Of course I would embrace her,
reassure her we'd be reunited,
but I felt the blow before it happened,
that just saying it would make it so.

She expressed the same fear that day
Bess and I sailed for Hamburg from the Hoboken Docks,
boarding the *Kronprinzessin Cecilie* –
the Crownprincess Cecilia, so fitting;
it seemed a good omen.
We were off to Scandinavia, performances booked
in Denmark and Sweden, including one
at the royal palace in Stockholm, for King Gustav V.

Mama eased the weight in my heart
when she asked me to bring her
a pair of warm woolen slippers, size 6,
when we returned from our trip:
she *did* believe in our reunion!

While we were away, she'd be with Dash
("Hardeen, the Great Sensation of Two Hemispheres"),
booked for two weeks on the Jersey shore,
performances at the Lyric Theater in Asbury Park.
They checked into the Imperial Hotel
a week after Bess and I set sail.

That's where she suffered the stroke.

Bess and I were in Copenhagen.
I'd performed at the Circus Beketow,
two Danish princes in attendance,
when the news came:
she died July 17, three days after her stroke.

I fainted when I read the cable.
My dear little mother – my poor little mama!

Burying Mama

After I recovered from the shock,
I cabled Dash to delay Mama's funeral
until Bess and I could get to New York.
Jewish burials usually take place immediately,
but I had to see Mama one last time.
My brothers and sister agreed to the delay.

Twelve days after she died –
the date of her death, July 17, would always wound me,
exactly one month after her birthday –
I went straight from the boat –
we'd returned on the same *Kronprinzessen Cecilie* –
to 278, where Mama lay in state, in the parlor.
She looked so dainty there, so restful.
I sat up with her all that night.

The next day we buried her in the family plot
in the Machpelah Cemetery, in Queens,
right next to Papa.
During my long night's vigil,
I'd placed the wool slippers into her casket,
the ones I'd bought for her in Bremen, size 6.

Soliloquy

I who have laughed at the terrors of death,
who have leapt from high bridges,
wriggled free from straitjackets underwater,
faced down the Russian secret police,
have received the shock of my life,
from which recovery may not be possible.
July 17 is always on my mind.
Can there ever be an escape?

I can't seem to get over it.
When a calm moment arrives,
I am suddenly overwhelmed.
It's as bad as it ever was.

If God ever permitted an angel
to walk the earth in human form,
it was my Mother.

Aftermath

After the funeral,
I stopped working for an entire month,
visited Mama's grave every day.
I read through every letter
she had written me since 1900,
had them transcribed, bound in a book.

Bess and I sailed again for Hamburg,
but in December I had to cancel
the performances I'd booked in Paris,
Bess and I going to Nice instead,
hoping for distraction on the Riviera.

I gambled in a Monte Carlo casino,
but it was the nearby cemetery
at the base of the promontory
called Tête de Chien
reserved for suicides who'd lost everything,
that captured my morbid imagination.

The Italian nobleman who hanged himself from a palm tree,
the despondent gamblers who'd drunk carbolic acid,
jumped from seaside cliffs or hotel room windows,
the young lovers who'd asphyxiated themselves
with charcoal fumes,
the Parisian woman who strangled her two children
before stabbing herself:
all for the loss of money, for financial ruin,
while I have lost so much more!

Spirits

Back from Europe, about a month from Mama's *yahrzeit*,
I found I just couldn't stay at 278,
Mama's memory in the walls,
the floor, the ceilings, the windows,
all over the brownstone.
Bess and I moved in with Dash in Flatbush.

I designed a granite memorial to my parents,
the name "Weiss" carved in the stone.
"Houdini" would be chiseled over it after I was dead.

Only days after we returned,
Archduke Ferdinand of Austria and his wife
assassinated in Sarajevo, and all my plans
up in smoke like a disappearing act.

We'd sailed back on the SS *Imperator*,
the former president, Theodore Roosevelt –
the "Colonel," as he preferred to be addressed –
likewise a passenger;
he'd recently explored the Amazon region.

I'd maneuvered the Colonel into requesting a séance
as part of the entertainment I provided,
then arranged to have the "spirits"
draw a map of the river
in response to his question:
"Where was I last Christmas?"

Gobsmacked along with the rest of the audience,
the Colonel asked me the next day
if he'd witnessed "genuine Spiritualism."

"No, Colonel," I told him,
"it was just hocus pocus."

Death Wish

I was back at Hammerstein's Roof Garden
where I'd debuted the Water Torture Cell
in America (the first public performance
was at the Cardiff Empire in Great Britain).
This time I unveiled Walking through a Brick Wall,
a huge hit. As *Billboard* wrote, the audience
"sat spellbound, too dumbfounded to applaud."

On the same bill, my Double Fold Death Defying Mystery,
in which the milk can pupa I was coffined up in
nestled in its own chrysalis, a large wooden crate,
another casket from which I emerged soaking wet.

To promote my Hammerstein's run,
I did a "Daring Dive" off the Battery,
at the southern tip of Manhattan,
handcuffed and leg-ironed,
nailed up in a packing crate, belted with steel bands.
Fifteen thousand people came to see me survive –
or not.

I felt like a fickle lover courting death,
knowing Mama was on the other side, waiting.

Houdinizing

My first suspended straitjacket escape?
Kansas City, September, 1915.
A couple of detectives strapped me into
"the strongest straitjacket owned by the KCPD."

Three months later a hundred thousand people
watched me do the same in Washington, DC,
and a week later up in Baltimore,
reporters in the *Baltimore Sun* building
peering through office windows
while I dangled like a bug from a spider's thread
a hundred feet above the intersection
of Charles and Baltimore Streets.

My stunts got more outrageous.
In Fort Worth I was dragged behind a motorcycle,
freeing myself from handcuffs.

And back at the Hippodrome in New York?
I made an elephant disappear!

Funk & Wagnalls would include the word "Houdinize"
in the dictionary, by 1920:
"To release or extricate oneself by wriggling out."

Special Powers

Years ago when Bess and I were just getting started,
we did a mind-reading act for the California Concert Company.
I was Professor Harry Houdini, the Great Mystifier,
Bess Mlle. Beatrice Houdini, the Celebrated Clairvoyant.
She made "spiritual forms" materialize.

The trick was electrifying; word spread,
the house packed like a suitcase,
but I felt like such a fraud.
The audience really believed we communicated
with their dead loved ones.
Their credulity filled me with guilt.
I'd made a game of the reverence
they regarded their departed loved ones with.
I realized this bordered on crime,
playing with their mourning,
their hopes in an afterlife,
reuniting with their dead.
We had to stop performing that act:
it was simply unconscionable.

Even when I tricked the Colonel
about the spirits knowing about his Amazon adventures,
I felt I had to tell him the truth,
not that I ever revealed my tricks.

Still, I didn't think it wrong
to let the legend of my special powers spread,
though at times the situation was most awkward.
The great actress, Sarah Bernhardt, performing in Boston,
attended my show at the B.F. Keith Building on Tremont,
astounded by my straitjacket escape.

I'd met her a few weeks before in New York,
when she was performing at the Met.
We returned to the hotel together,
and in the car, she asked me
if I would restore her amputated leg!
She really believed I had superhuman powers!

The Rabbis' Sons' Benevolent Association

With Al Jolson and Irving Berlin, I organized
the Rabbis' Sons' Theatrical Benevolent Association,
to give benefit performances to support the troops,
once America got into the war.
Amazing, the number of Jewish entertainers onstage
who'd had rabbis and cantors for fathers!
The Shubert Brothers, the Warner Brothers, the list goes on.
As Minnie Marx put it,
the mother and manager of the Marx Brothers,
"Where else can people who don't know anything
make so much money?"

I raised money for the Red Cross,
trained soldiers to escape from German handcuffs,
sold tons of Liberty bonds,
even registered for the draft,
though I was already forty-three.
I did entertain the troops with my magic
in the army camps around the country.

When a German U-Boat torpedoed
the SS *Antilles* in the North Atlantic,
killing sixty-seven U.S. servicemen,
we staged a sensational benefit at the Hippodrome,
which I promoted with a suspended straitjacket escape
in Times Square, sixty feet over Broadway and Seventh.

How I'd loved all things German,
but I was an American, first.

The Silver Screen

Face it, vaudeville was giving way to the cinema
(not to mention radio),
and the war had put a stop to my transatlantic tours.
As far back as 1907 my Weighlock Bridge jump
into the Erie Canal'd been filmed,
my exploits captured forever on celluloid,
and a couple of years later Cinema Lux
made a feature film of some of my stunts,
Merveilleux exploits de Houdini à Paris.

My big mistake was investing in a movie company,
the Film Development Corporation.
It was my first foray into the world of business.
We never turned a profit.

I convinced Dash to stop performing as Hardeen,
take over management of the business.
For half a dozen years the FDC gave me headaches.
Dash developed ulcers, even worse. It was a mess
of lawsuits, countersuits, real estate debacles.
We invested thousands but never made a dime.

The only good thing about it?
It was why I went into pictures myself!

The Master of Mystery

In 1918, Octagon Films released *The Master Mystery*,
a silent film serialized in fifteen parts,
in which I played Quentin Locke,
an undercover Justice Department agent,
battling an international cartel called International Patents,
Inc.,
always ambushed by thugs, escaping from
straitjackets, barbed wire, nets, electric chairs,
constantly saving Eva Brent (Marguerite Marsh)
from the Automaton (first ever robot in the movies),
escape the major dramatic theme.

Each episode ended as a cliffhanger,
Eve or me trussed up and facing certain death,
then a card announcing:
"The continuation of the HOUDINI SERIAL
will be shown at this theater NEXT WEEK."

The Master Mystery was a huge hit.
The war was over.
Everyone wanted to celebrate!

The trouble for me was, I had to sue
to get the half of the net profits I was promised.
The case dragged on for four years.
By the time the court awarded me $33,000,
the production company was bankrupt.

The Movies

Altogether I starred in five films over five years,
The Grim Game, Terror Island, The Man from Beyond
(*L'homme du passé* in France),
Haldane of the Secret Service, the other four,
playing Harvey Hanford, Harry Harper, Howard Hillary,
Heath Haldane: all characters with H.H. initials.

I wrote the screenplay for *The Man from Beyond,*
which ends in a climactic rescue scene at Niagara Falls,
but plays on reincarnation, the Second Coming.
The ultimate escape, indeed.
I was still dreaming of a reunion
with Mama, in Heaven.

Howard Hillary's brought back to life
after spending a hundred years frozen in a block of ice.
Spiritualism was popular. Conan Doyle's
The New Revelation makes a cameo appearance.
"The very best sensational movie I have ever seen,"
Sir Arthur blurbed, his ego stroked,
"It holds one breathless."

We lost more money during our Hollywood interlude
than we made, assets vanishing like Jennie the elephant
from the Hippodrome stage!

As I told the American magician Karl Germain
("Germain the Wizard"),
"*No* illusion is good in a film.
We simply resort to camera tricks."
Where's the danger? What's the risk?

My Wild Oat

Now comes the hard part.
Mama'd been gone five years,
so I can't use that as an excuse,
even if I still missed her every day.

And Bess? I never stopped being devoted to her,
leaving little notes – "Adorable Sunshine" –
on her pillow or the kitchen counter.
We were a team, professionally and romantically.

Bess and Mama? They loved one another,
but as I told Bess, "I love you
as I shall never again love any woman,
but the love for a mother is a love
that only a true mother ought to possess."

But the story of my shame begins in 1915,
when I met Jack London and his wife Charmian,
in Oakland, when I was performing at the Orpheum,
Charmian quite taken with me.
She sent me a copy of her book,
The Log of the Snark, about their South Pacific voyage,
inscribed to "Charming Houdini," adding,
"I will never forget you."

Then, a year to the day I met them backstage at the Orpheum,
Jack died, kidney failure, only forty,
the result of all that hard living,
Klondike hardships, tropical diseases, heavy drinking.

Over a year later, while I was at the Hippodrome, 1918,
Charmian had an apartment in the Village, Washington Place,

where it all began. She told me I "stirred her to the deeps,"
called me her "Magic Lover," her "Magic Man."

In return I wrote, "Now I know how kings
have given up their kingdoms for a woman,"
and the ultimate declaration of love:
"I would have told her – my mother – about you."
But I just couldn't continue the affair.

In June, 1919, I organized a lavish twenty-fifth reunion party
at the Hotel Alexandria in LA, complete
with Mendelssohn's *Wedding March*
as Bess and I made our entrance.

Did Bess know about Charmian? We never talked about it,
but surely others wagged their tongues.
I was so deeply ashamed if I hurt her.
While we danced at the Alexandria, I passed Bess a note:
"If only my Sainted Mother were here,
how she would nod her head with pride."

Elementary

Our final trip abroad, once peace reigned again,
a six-month tour of Great Britain,
felt as much like a victory lap as a reunion.
We packed the theaters wherever we went –
Edinburgh, Glasgow, London, Nottingham, Hull.
For a two-week booking at the London Palladium,
I made the record-setting sum of $3,750 per week!
I could attract the public without killing myself,
usually performing just a single escape trick –
the Chinese Water Torture Cell – and lecturing otherwise,
boasting about my exploits and movies.
Fame has its rewards, even if some critics complained.

The Magicians' Club honored me with a banquet
at the Savoy in London.
Bess and I sailed home in July,
aboard *The Imperator*, the same ship on which
I'd met and entertained the Colonel – Roosevelt –
six years earlier, just weeks before
the Archduke was assassinated and the world changed.

The high point of the trip?
Meeting Sir Arthur Conan Doyle, creator of Sherlock Holmes
–
Holmes, the epitome of rational logic! –
who encouraged me to explore that murky,
 faith-based realm of the pseudo-religion of Spiritualism.
The game was afoot, as Holmes said to Watson.

Spiritualism

Professional magicians have always been at war
with Spiritualists. As I told a reporter
for the *Los Angeles Times,*
"It takes a flimflammer to catch a flimflammer."

The Spiritualist hoax began a generation before I was born
in Hydesville, New York, 1848, two sisters,
Catherine and Margaret Fox, claiming
they'd established contact with a mysterious spirit.
Soon they and their sister were charging admission
to flocks of gullible marks, anxious to see "spirits" at work.

Soon enough, mediums were sprouting like
mushrooms after a rainstorm –
just as much a fungus, too –
claiming "scientific" proof of immortality:
spirits passing from earthly life
to some mystical "Summerland" beyond,
from which they visited the living at will.
A cruel hoax on grieving loved ones.

Robert-Houdin exposed those quacks
who used magic tricks
in the name of the supernatural.
The Scottish magician, John Henry Anderson, also
challenged Spiritualists, showing their shabby tricks.
"I caused my table to rap as loud as any of theirs!"

The English conjurer, J.N. Maskelyne, likewise
exposed their tricks on stage, catching
Ira and William Davenport red-handed.
Robert Heller and H.S. Lynne pulled away

the glittery curtain, revealing the charlatans.
The great American magician, Harry Kellar,
who'd worked as an assistant to the Davenport Brothers,
also exposed the Spiritualists' methods,
especially the Davenports' signature rope-tie release;
levitation, table-turning, direct-writing –
all the tricks of the Spiritualist trade.

Maybe it was professional pride,
watching the mediums fleece the flocks
from fraudulent claims, tarnishing the integrity
of legitimate magical tricks.

But why did I care so much?
I hated the way these dimestore frauds
played on the vulnerabilities of their followers.
I yearned so much to speak with Mama,
knowing it was impossible in this life,
infuriated by the cruelty, taking advantage of grief.
Fakery demeans mourning, and mourning is sacred.

Meeting the Doyles

I was performing at the Brighton Hippodrome that April
when I went to Windlesham Manor
to have lunch with Conan Doyle and his wife
at their East Sussex country home.
We'd been corresponding for some weeks
about Spiritualism. I'd sent him a copy
of *The Unmasking of Robert-Houdin*,
which the Freudians had once again called "Oedipal" –
slaying the father; the man from whom I'd taken my name.

It was those con artists the Davenport Brothers
we mainly discussed. I'd noted in my book,
"all their work was skillful manipulation,
not spiritualist manifestations," Doyle objecting
he considered them "the greatest mediums of their kind."

Sir Arthur was a generous chap, if naïve and gullible,
every inch the perfect English gentleman.
He'd lost his son in the war,
shot in the neck at the Somme,
dead two years later from the Spanish Flu.
Lady Conan Doyle – his second wife – lost her brother
at the battle of the Mons.

They so desperately wanted to make contact
with the spirits of their dead.
What sort of churl was I,
to throw cold water on their hopes?
Still, I could do no more than politely demur,
profess myself an agnostic.
Our break, alas, would come later.

Mediums

The press covered everything we did,
nothing private about our differences of opinion,
which sometimes made our conversations awkward,
Sir Arthur as sweet as any mortal I've ever known,
but oh, so credulous for all his courtesy!

I'd attended a séance with Anna Brittain,
who Doyle claimed put him in touch with Kingsley,
his son who'd died at twenty-five just two years earlier.
I found Brittain's tricks ridiculous, the "spiritual portraits"
and all the rest, the images of the dead
who'd "passed into the Spirit."

But Sir Arthur extolled her powers.
He called Spiritualism his "sacred cause,"
sure he'd been appointed by the divine
to be a "torch bearer":
his two books, *The New Revelation* and *The Vital Message*,
mapping out our relations with "the Unseen."

And then Lady Conan Doyle developed
her own "mediumistic powers":
a special talent for automatic writing.
In a trance, she became a conduit
for the voices of the dead,
her hand scrawling their messages across the page.
Had she convinced herself this was legitimate?
Was it devotion to her husband's mission?

Sir Arthur even suggested my magic act
derived from supernatural sources.
"My dear chap," he wrote to me,
"why do you seek demonstrations of the occult
when you are giving one all the time?"

Ectoplasm

Not that I bought all of my rabbi father's teachings,
or felt in any way bound by Jewish law,
but the Torah forbids séances in no uncertain terms:
no pithom sorcerers, no necromancers (*Deuteronomy* 18).
"Let no one among you consult with the dead."

The mediums' tricks that hooked Sir Arthur?
Tilting tables, auras, flying objects, speaking in tongues,
the sticky ectoplasm coming from the medium's orifices –
mouth, nose, ears, navel, vagina –
physical proof of spiritual presence.

But what he really craved,
the summoning of a voice from beyond the grave,
some "personal" message to show contact had been made,
itself proof of immortality, of the closeness
of the dead to the living.

To humor my friend I attended another half dozen séances,
these with a French medium called Eva C.
Held at the Society for Psychical Research in London,
they lasted over three hours, Eva oozing ectoplasm
like toothpaste from a collapsible tube, all the proof
Sir Arthur needed. I found her a fraud,
but all I wrote him, before we sailed home in July:
"I have had some interesting sittings during my stay.
I thoroughly enjoyed them."

The American Mission

Two years after our tour of Great Britain,
the Doyles came to America, Sir Arthur here
to spread the word about Spiritualism,
lecturing to a sold-out Carnegie Hall about
the spirit self, the "etheric body," surviving death,
reuniting with deceased loved ones,
the happiness in the afterlife.
"Doyle Says Marital Relations OK in Next World,"
the *New York Herald* headline screamed.

Sir Arthur's "evidence" was mainly personal stories,
his encounters with his own dead relatives,
"spirit photographs" projected on a screen,
ghosts captured on the photographic plate,
though invisible to the living eye.
A photo of himself, seated in a chair,
his son Kingsley hovering in the air beside him.

Also projected on the screen,
Cenotaph spirit photos at an Armistice Day rally
taken by Ada Emma Deane, a medium,
the faces of fallen soldiers floating in an etheric cloud,
a hoax the *Daily Sketch* exposed
in London two years later,
pointing out the visages of living athletes
hovering over the crowd.

We'd maintained a friendly correspondence,
lighthearted and loving, while separated by the Atlantic.
Sir Arthur's honesty never in question,
I only wondered how he could be fooled by fraudsters,
this creator of Sherlock Holmes,

the logical detective who never had the wool
pulled over his eyes.
He labeled this evangelical tour
his "American Mission."

The Séance

Six weeks into Arthur's successful American tour –
I'd been following him in the newspapers –
the Doyles came to lunch at 278.
Sir Arthur presented me with an autographed copy
of his latest book, *The Wanderings of a Spiritualist*,
and I entertained him in the library
with an elaborate show of "spirit writing,"
Doyle, astounded, insisting
I must have employed "psychic means,"
while I assured him it was all trickery and nothing else.
Never having been taught the artifices of conjuring,
it was easy to gain his confidence, hoodwink him.

In return for our hospitality, several weeks later,
the Doyles invited Bess and me for a weekend
in Atlantic City; they were staying at the beach
in the posh Ambassador Hotel.

On Sunday, Sir Arthur approached us
as we lounged on the beach, inviting me
(but not Bess, whom he pointedly excluded)
to an automatic-writing séance
in which Lady Conan Doyle promised to summon
the spirit of my mother, Cecilia Weiss,
now nine years gone.

Did she have pure intentions?
Was she only offering comfort,
knowing how I missed my mother?
But Lady Conan Doyle's ham-handed writing
only offended me, stung like a poisonous insect.

"Oh my darling, at last I am through. I am happy.
Now I can rest in peace.
God bless you, Sir Arthur,
for what you have done for us, putting us in touch
with our beloved ones on the earth plane,"
Lady Conan Doyle scrawled in her trance,
my mother's "spirit" insisting upon her happiness,
on the Doyles "bridging the gap,"
through fifteen pages of platitudinous drivel.

But this so-called "message"?
Nothing specific about our relationship,
the communication written in English,
a language my mother never learned to speak –
or to write.

This séance drove us apart as surely
as a wedge prying apart wood.
Doyle hadn't deliberately tried to fool me,
but his "magnanimity" galled me.
I should *thank* him and his wife?
But we would remain "friends."
I hadn't yet the nerve
to let them know.

The Rift

I escorted the Doyles to the pier
when they sailed for England the end of June,
posed for farewell photos onboard the RMS *Adriatic*,
had a bon-voyage bouquet placed in his cabin.

But I'd had it with the mystic mumbo-jumbo,
especially offended by the so-called séance,
playing on my emotions for my mother,
the mourning that continued
to tinge my every thought.

In October, I wrote a piece for the *New York Sun*, declaring,
"In my twenty-five years of investigation,
the hundreds of séances I've attended,
nothing has ever convinced me
there's any possibility of communicating
with the loved ones who have gone beyond."

Doyle's disappointment at the implication
the Atlantic City séance was a sham
manifested as a complaint
I'd impugned Lady Conan Doyle's integrity.
"I know the purity of my wife's mediumship," he avowed.
While I explained the reasons for my skepticism
and assured him I held both of them
"in the highest esteem,"
the damage was done, our friendship over.

A Psychic Diogenes

Arthur came to my show at the Orpheum in Denver
the next time he brought his family to America,
and Bess attended Doyle's lecture
at the smaller Ogden Theater.
We aimed for civility, but I couldn't let him
influence public opinion, and certainly,
given his fame,
his word went much farther than mine.

So two weeks later, in California,
I told a reporter from the *Oakland Tribune*
Doyle had repeatedly been duped
by discredited mediums,
an article titled "Houdini Unmasks the Mediums."
Naturally, Sir Arthur was angry,
demanded an apology.
Now the breach could never be repaired.

With my usual fervor I began a crusade
to debunk Spiritualism, unmasking bogus mediums.
I toured the Midwest, lecturing at universities.
I published *A Magician Among the Spirits*,
believing it my duty,
for the betterment of humanity,
to tell the public frankly
about my investigations into Spiritualism.
I even sent Sir Arthur a copy,
to which he did not respond.

One of the newspapers dubbed me
"a psychic Diogenes,"
after the founder of Cynic philosophy,

and you know what?
I liked the idea of being an educator
as well as an entertainer.

The *Scientific American*

When the prestigious *Scientific American* announced
two cash prizes to anyone who could provide
"conclusive psychic manifestations" –
i.e., a legitimate medium –
the magazine appointed a five-judge committee
to evaluate the "occult manifestations," including me,
along with the chair of Harvard's psychology department.
I loved being with real "learned professors,"
even as I worried these *luftmensches*
might be easily fooled by slick con artists.
Doyle, of course, was displeased, complaining
I could never be "impartial" –
which for him meant "credulous."
The newspapers called it "The Great Spirit Hunt."

Most mediums were just second-rate illusionists.
Anything they could do, I could do better –
and without "supernatural assistance."
They were laughable amateurs
in their gloomy séance rooms,
putting on dilettante shows under the cover of darkness.
It was downright insulting. Tawdry.

A parade of candidates came forward
over the next year and a half
after *Scientific American* announced its prize.
The "jolly medium" was one, a tubby pretender
named George Valentine, who claimed to be in touch
with a Native American spirit called Kokum.
Another was "the Boy Medium," Nino Pecoraro,
who caused objects to fly about during his séances,
speaking in the hoarse voice of "Palladino,"
the Italian spirit he channeled.

Some committee members were impressed –
until I trussed the boy up with rope,
and all he could do was summon Palladino's raspy voice.
Pathetic.

But it was the graceful Mina Crandon of Beacon Hill
who made the greatest claim for the $2,500 prize.

The Blonde Witch of Lime Street

Mina Crandon – aka, Margery –
came to the committee's attention in 1923
when McDougall, the Harvard psychology professor,
fell under her spell, began attending her Beacon Hill séances,
along with J. Malcolm Bird,
an editor at the *Scientific American*,
who likewise became Mina's Lime Street lodger,
and the Brit., Hereward Carrington,
who became her lover.
All were bewitched by her Circe-charm and beauty.

Bird almost awarded Mina the prize behind my back,
enthusiastically summarizing her séances
in the *Scientific American*.
He'd even suggested her *Nom de Séance*, Margery.
"Margery Passes All Psychic Tests,"
the *New York Times* headline crowed
after Bird's fawning evaluation.

So I came to Boston, attended a Lime Street séance,
yanking their leads to slow the dogs down,
Bird later driving me to the Copley Plaza Hotel,
which was when I let him know Margery was a charlatan.
"One more sitting and I will expose everything."
Of course, Bird went back to Lime Street,
wagging his tail, told Margery everything I'd said.

Mina'd met her future husband Le Roi Crandon,
a wealthy Boston surgeon, when she was his patient
at Dorchester Hospital, suffering from an appendicitis.
Though already married to a grocer,
she seduced Doctor Crandon, divorced her husband,

moved into the swank Beacon Hill house
a few blocks from the Boston Public Garden.

Three years into their marriage,
when Dr. Crandon developed an interest in Spiritualism,
Mina's mediumistic talents suddenly revealed themselves –
table-tilting in their fourth-floor library,
channeling the voice of her dead older brother Walter,
the *Boston Herald* describing the ghost's persona
as "vivid, sharply defined and unforgettable."
Witty, ribald, irreverent Walter,
who'd died in a railroad accident
a dozen years before, had an ability
"for a quick retort or a cutting phrase,"
reciting limericks and cracking wise.

And of course Sir Arthur sang her praises
when the Crandons crossed the Atlantic
to meet with European psychic "experts,"
claiming Margery's authenticity
"beyond all question."

Margery at the Charlesgate

We held the next séance at Daniel Comstock's apartment
in the Charlesgate Hotel near Governor Square,
a turreted building that looked like a haunted castle,
Comstock, an MIT physicist, another committee member.

When the lights were out, I caught Margery cheating,
tilting the table by stretching forward and down,
her head stuck underneath it, the fraud exposed!
But Bird was a *traitor*, excusing Margery
like a fawning courtier.
We agreed to three more séances in August,
another chance for Margery to redeem herself.
"Margery to Rassle with the Handcuff King,"
the *Boston Herald* headline promised.

"Houdini, you goddamn son of a bitch,"
Margery growled in "Walter's" voice,
the spirit of her dead brother,
at Comstock's Charlesgate apartment
the next time we met.
"I put a curse on you now that will follow you
every day until you die."

But nothing happened at these séances. Why?
I'd confined her in "Houdini's Box,"
a specially constructed cabinet,
only Margery's head and arms protruding,
unable to do her tricks.
Scientific American did not award a prize
or declare Margery a true medium.
"Houdini Routs Pet Spook of Science,"
the *New York Mirror* proclaimed.

Bird tried discrediting me by "revealing"
that I was a Jew. Conan Doyle did the same,
calling me "as Oriental as our own Disraeli."
Even Margery'd sing-songed in Walter's voice,
"Harry Houdini, he sure is a sheeny."

But who got the last laugh?
After my lecture at the New York Police Academy
on "How to Catch Fake Spiritualists,"
Edmund Wilson praised me in the *New Republic*,
a highbrow intellectual journal.
Sweet vindication!
Take *that*, you anti-Semitic frauds!

CODA:

Escape

Alternative Facts II

How did my husband die?
Not even I can tell you that.
Or at least I can't make sense of it.
The facts? He was performing
at the Princess Theater in Montreal,
when three McGill students came
to his dressing room, October 22, 1926.
Harry'd invited one of them, Sam Smilovitz,
to paint his portrait. Harry'd admired
some of Sam's sketches
from the speech at the podium.

A strapping boy named Gordon Whitehead,
there with Sam, asked Harry if he could resist
the hardest blow struck to the abdomen.
Odd question. Harry demurred,
offered to let Whitehead
feel his muscled forearm, but Whitehead insisted.
Four or five blows to Harry's midsection
staggered him like a Nitro Express rifle
blasting into an African elephant's hide!

But Harry finished his last Montreal show
the next day, boarded the night train to Detroit,
feverish as a sick animal.
When he became worse and worse, I wired
for a doctor to meet us in the morning,
the train wailing across Ontario,
foreboding as a banshee.

The doctor examined Harry in his dressing room
at the Garrick Theater, pronounced acute appendicitis,
Harry's temperature having spiked to 102.
But Harry insisted on performing his show,

the Garrick sold out; he wouldn't let the audience down –
even as his fever hit 104 when the curtain rose on Act 1.

Even when the show finished, Harry refused
the ambulance waiting at the stage-door,
hailed a taxi back to the Statler Hotel
where he insisted on calling his doctor
in New York, for a second opinion,
even though Kennedy, the head of surgery at Grace Hospital,
had explained the urgency
when he saw Harry at 3:00 that morning.

My poor Harry! By the time they operated,
it was far too late. This time he'd blown his escape.
Peritonitis had already set in.
He died six days later, on Halloween.

But had Whitehead's sucker punch ruptured his appendix?
That was over a week before he died.
Not even Harry could have survived that long,
the medical experts told us.

Perhaps his appendix had burst onstage at the Garrick.
I had a $25,000 double indemnity insurance policy
from New York Life riding on an accidental death.
Harry's lawyer Bernard Ernst got them to pay.

Of course, that insufferable prig Conan Doyle
crowed that the "spirit world"
had been "incensed" against Harry,
as if this were a comic book melodrama, his death
"most certainly decreed by the other side."
What a tedious blowhard Sir Arthur had become!
Was this the curse of Margery's "Walter" come true, then?

We buried my beloved in the Machpelah family plot,
laid him to rest with his sainted Mama and Papa.

The Great Escape

Harry and I had a code
in case I ever tried contacting him
through a medium, after he died.
The code involved the word "Rosabelle,"
the song I was singing on Coney Island,
as part of the Floral Sisters,
the night we met.

For years I tried,
attending a séance every Halloween,
but of course I never succeeded.
After ten years, a "Final Houdini Séance"
on the roof of the Knickerbocker Hotel in Hollywood,
I stopped trying, knowing it was useless,
though I did ask Harry's friend,
Walter Gibson, to carry on the tradition.

After he died, I found the letter
he'd written to me that began,
"Sweetheart, when you read this I shall be dead,"
which put a lump in my throat, tears blinding me.

"I shall be at rest by the side of my beloved parents,"
he went on, "and wait for you always – remember!"

I knew all about Charmian London, of course,
but he confessed to loving only two women in his life,
his sainted mother Cecilia and me.
"Yours in Life, Death and Ever After."

Would we ever meet? I wondered, remembering
the letter I wrote to Sir Arthur.

"It was Houdini himself that was the secret,"
I'd explained, no need for "psychic help"
to perform his escapes.

Ah, escape!
Every escape is a success story, no?
Now you see me,
now you don't.

Acknowledgments

MockingOwl Roost: "Escape"
Off Course: "My Father Flees"
Trajectory: "The Rabbis' Sons' Benevolent Association" and
"The Silver Screen"

About the Author

Charles Rammelkamp is Prose Editor for BrickHouse Books in Baltimore, where he lives with his wife, Abby. The two are retired from federal government service. Rammelkamp is the author of several collections of "historical" or "biographical" poetry sequences, written in dramatic monologue form, including *Fusen Bakudan* (Time Being Books), about World War Two Japanese balloon bombs and leper colony missionaries in Vietnam; *Mata Hari: Eye of the Day* (Apprentice House), about the life and career of the World War I *femme fatale* spy; *American Zeitgeist* (Apprentice House), which deals with the populist politician and Scopes Trial buffoon, William Jennings Bryan; *Catastroika* (Apprentice House), another collection of dramatic monologues in the voices of Maria Rasputin, the mad monk's daughter, who escaped Russia after the Revolution and became a lion tamer for Ringling Brothers, and a fictional Jewish character, Sasha Federmesser, who likewise escapes and immigrates to Baltimore. A chapbook of poems about female sailors in the British Royal Navy during the 17th and 18th centuries, *Jack Tar's Lady Parts* (Main Street Rag Press), is also written in this style. A collection of poems about psychedelic drugs and yoga, the murky CIA mind-control programs of the mid-20th Century, titled *Transcendence,* has been accepted by BlazeVOX Books. Other poetry collections include *Ugler Lee* and *The Field of Happiness* (Kelsay Books) and *Mortal Coil,* a chapbook published by *Clare Songbirds.*

www.ingramcontent.com/pod-product-compliance
Lightning Source LLC
Chambersburg PA
CBHW022202080426
42734CB00006B/542